Artwork on Mind's Canvas

Artwork on Mind's Canvas

Copyright © 2017 Shelley Ann Vrgleski

All rights reserved. No part of this book may be reproduced or transmitted in any form or by any means, electronic or mechanical, including photocopying, recording, or by any information storage and retrieval system, without written permission of the publisher.

Zaimina Publishing
contact@zaiminapublishing.com

Book design, cover art and illustrations: © Shelley Ann Vrgleski
www.shelleyannvrgleski.com

ISBN Print (Trade PB): 978-0-9952125-1-0

Artwork on Mind's Canvas

Written & Illustrated by

Shelley Ann Vrgleski

ZAIMINA PUBLISHING

Stojo,

My best friend and inspiration,
with whom dreams are made

Contents

Chapter 1: Perception of Pain

- 3   What is this?
- 5   Trapped
- 7   Fragmented
- 9   Less
- 11   Junkie
- 13   Crackling Rain
- 15   Humanity
- 19   Comfort Zone: Breaking Out
- 21   Forget Me Not
- 23   Our Past and Future Selves
- 25   Bloodshot
- 27   War
- 29   Mud
- 31   Perfectly Imperfect Woman
- 33   All is Not Lost
- 37   Our Pride and Joy
- 39   I Write

Chapter 2: Perception of Pleasure

- 43   The Age
- 45   Fayre
- 47   Sens du Temps
- 49   Sweet Dove
- 51   Mariovo's Immortal Voice
- 53   Something New
- 55   Affaire des Levres
- 57   The Kiss
- 59   The Dawning
- 61   The Dance
- 63   Still, the Waters Call
- 71   I Write

CHAPTER 3: THOUGHT

- 74 Jeweled Pair
- 75 Feet: What Stories They Tell
- 76 Found
- 77 Summer's Dream
- 78 The Beach
- 79 Venus Fly Trap
- 80 Abandon
- 81 Corn Dog Grass
- 82 Last Night Being Single
- 83 Honey
- 84 Aiko's Nest
- 85 Little Monster
- 86 Love in the After-World
- 87 Supernatural Gloss
- 88 Forever Entwined
- 89 Garden
- 90 Eau de Redolence
- 91 Buried in Vines
- 92 Holiday
- 93 Full

TAKE-AWAY THOUGHT   95

ABOUT THE AUTHOR   97

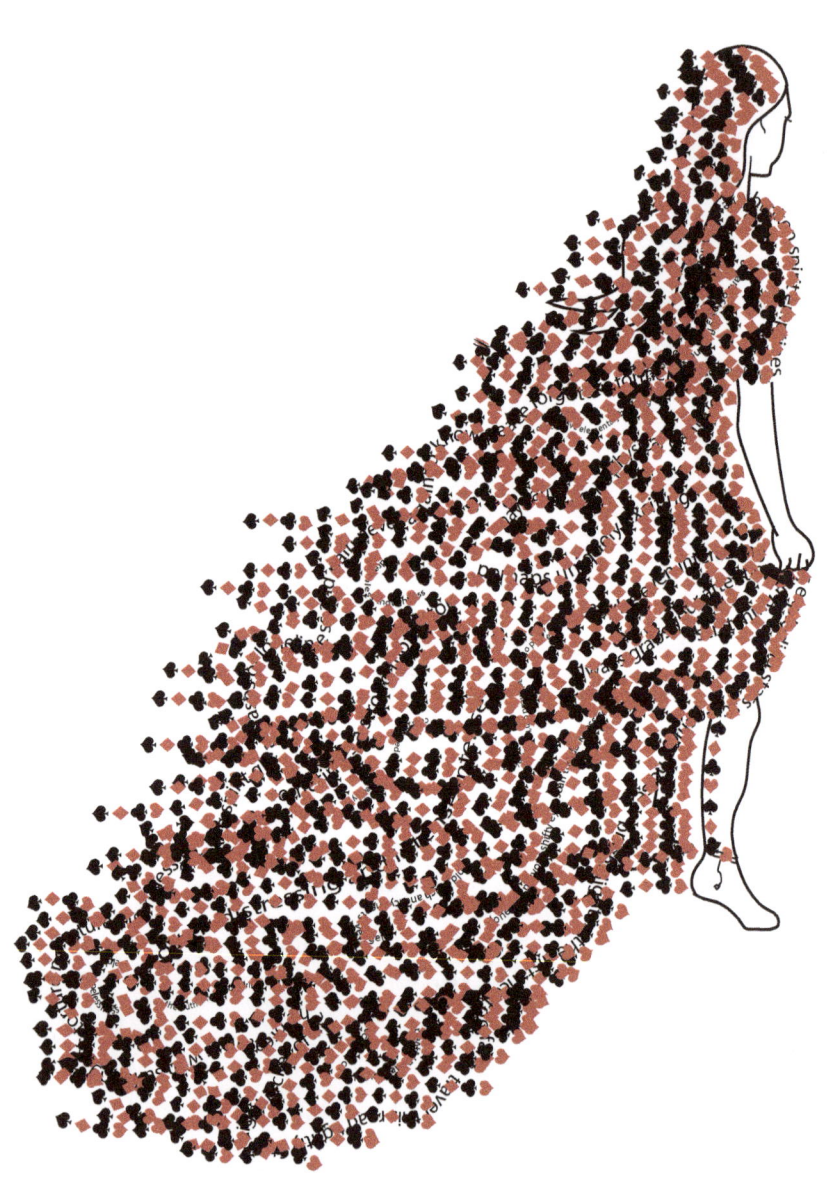

Chapter 1: Perception of Pain

Often distressing and intense
May cause some physical damage
Sometimes a strong motivator
Perhaps uniquely exciting
Maybe even interesting
But always grabs your attention.

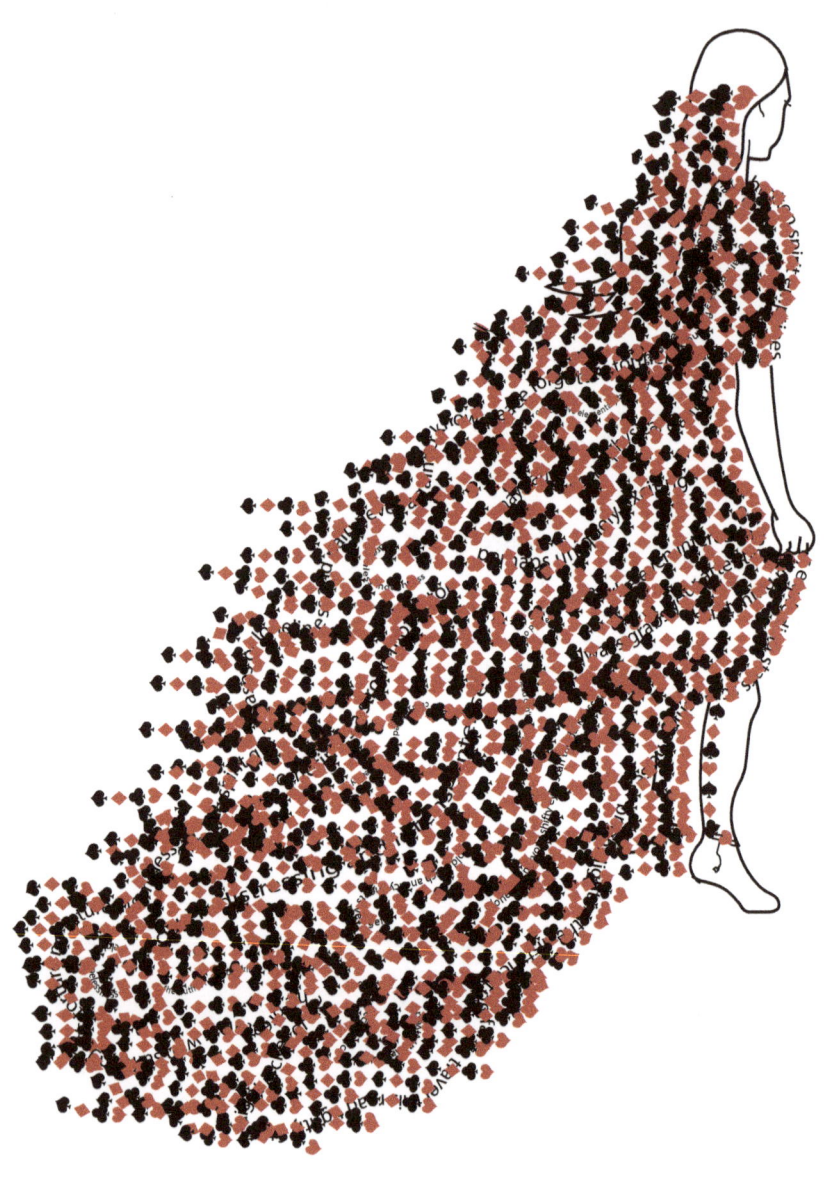

What is this?

noise
screeching
scratching nails
exploding stars
narrow passageway
bright light in the distance
too far to travel this road
tightly fit straight-jacket of ache
breathless with suffering, it's torture
please help me take it away forever

please help me take it away forever
no future, homeless, broken spirit
great gasps of loneliness and pain
never again to know peace
torrents of tears blaze trails
forgotten torment
ink laden mind
emptiness
alone
guilt

Trapped

alone and nervous at the window
crushing waves of anxiety
ISOLATION

shifting eyes scan the darkness
afraid of the truth
DECEPTION

icy rivers of torment
hurt and humiliation
CONFUSION

fate's empty promises
anger and longing
DESPERATION

refusing to surrender
hope amid chaos
INTIMIDATION

reflections on suicide
tsunami of tears
DEPRESSION

headlights in the driveway
curse of relief
REPUDIATION

calm acceptance, veil engaged
one more day
SURVIVED.

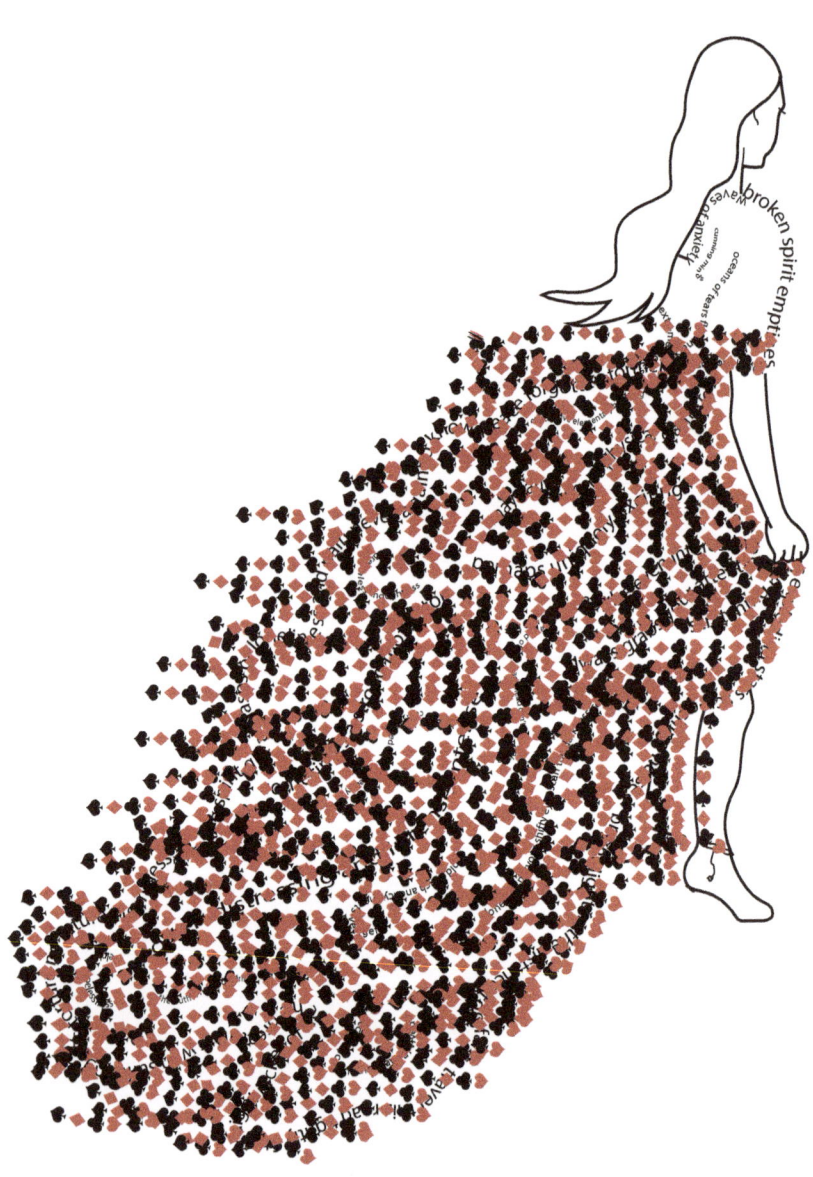

Fragmented

Who can explain emotions we feel?
Why do we care so deeply?
It is such pain to know this place
If only for moments briefly

Who are we but cells in a body
Our planet just one in a trillion
The air we breathe and food we eat
All things within our vision

This day we fear our emotions true
We hate what we don't understand
Our fists raised high to fight this war
Our words as sharp as weapons

Why do we fight this vicious battle?
For nought, tis certain we fear it
We are but one and the same in this world
Small wonder, we're fragmented spirit

We fight and kill for nothing good
Selfishness and fear to defeat us
To ignore the pain of this crazy life
Is to damn us to hell none the less.

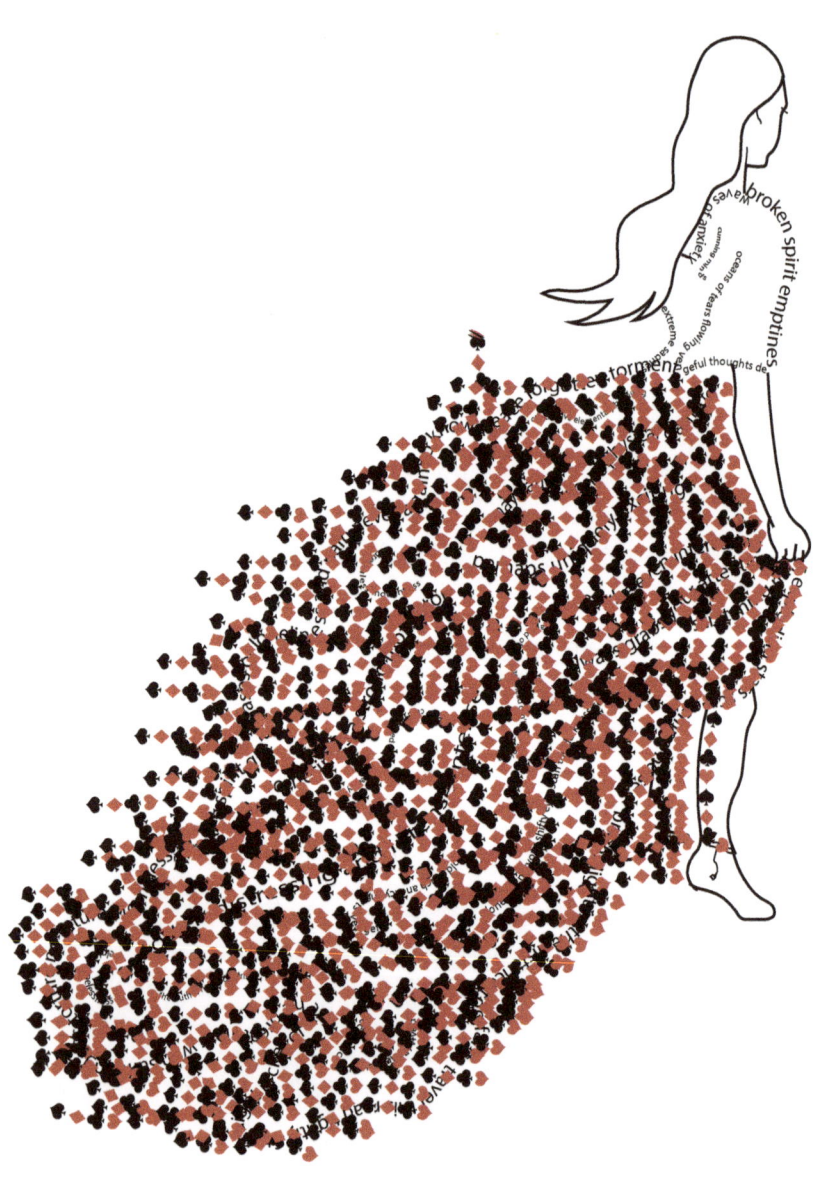

Less

Thoughtless

Dreamless

Helpless

Hopeless

Absent is our dreamless, thoughtless mind

Lost life for our helpless, hopeless kind.

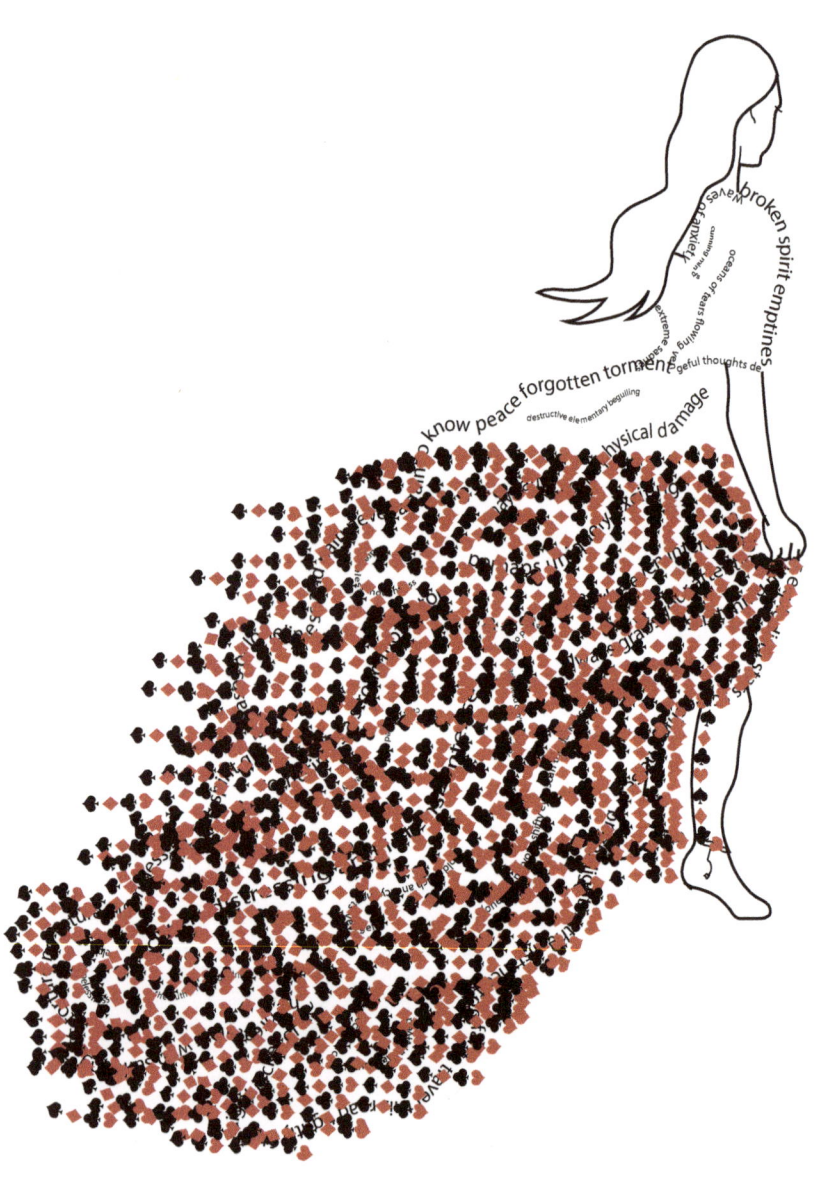

Junkie

Sweet and spicy
Its nectar calls
The taking of which exacts a price:
Your pride, your mind, your body, your soul.

See it trickle
It overflows
Warm heart to mouth, always fateful:
So pure and sweet, smooth as Bordeaux.

My dreams are red
There is no cure
My vein is open, rampantly bled:
Toxic juice, it's such a wicked lure.

For time will tell
Of my demise
If in the end my soul to sell
The buyer hell and I've arrived.

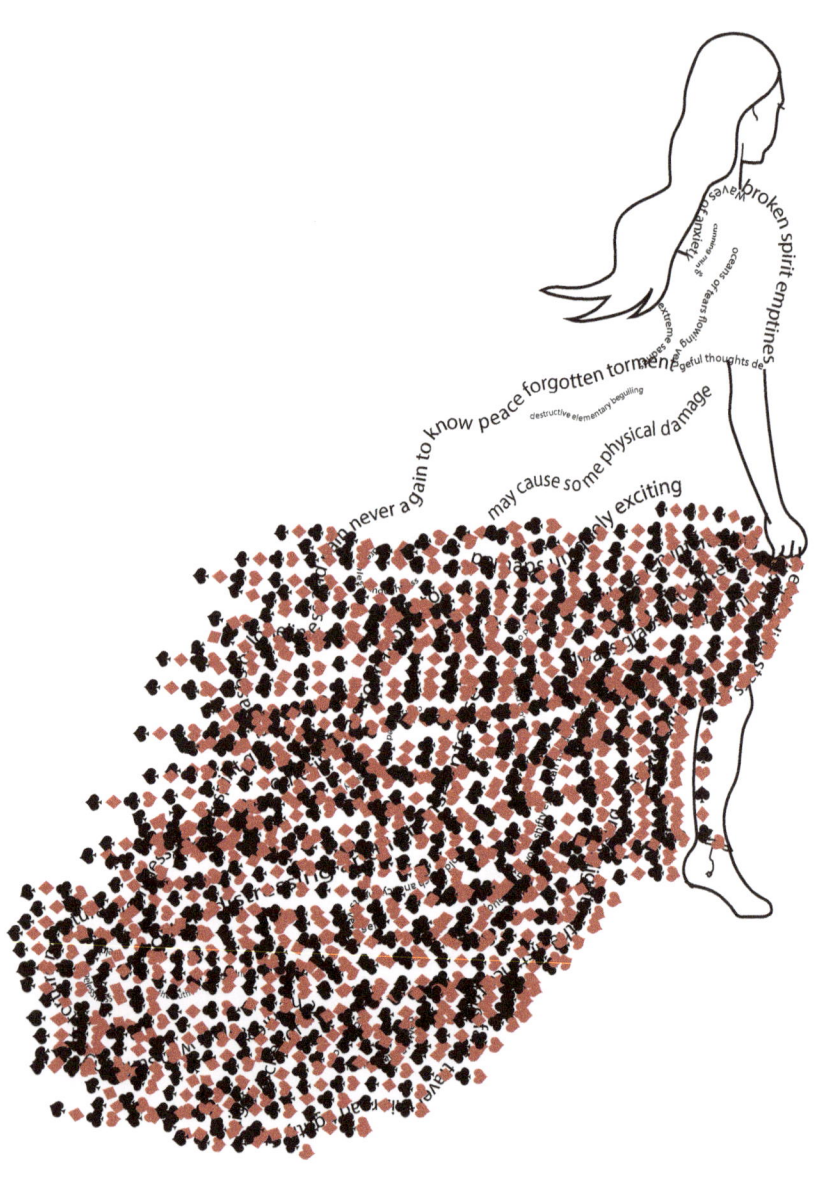

Crackling Rain

Cold-hearted soul…
Winter wonderland
oppressed by man

Humanity

Are we a superior race of beings?
More than anything we are confused
as history has taught—
    it's hard to believe.

What do we gain with fighting?
Only evil hearts and deception flourish
it seems with souls intact—
    the innocent pay the price.

Are there such beings of wisdom?
An infinitely impenetrable force
of constant energy—
    a pure and godly authority.

What can we accomplish?
Our people barely survive and
we care nothing of saving our race—
    change is difficult, people are dying.

Is it too late?
I fear time will tell
if all mankind will cease to exist—
    apocalypse may be inevitable.

Will we change in time?
Our small amount of wisdom
will let us see the devastating changes—
    failure to correct results in doom.

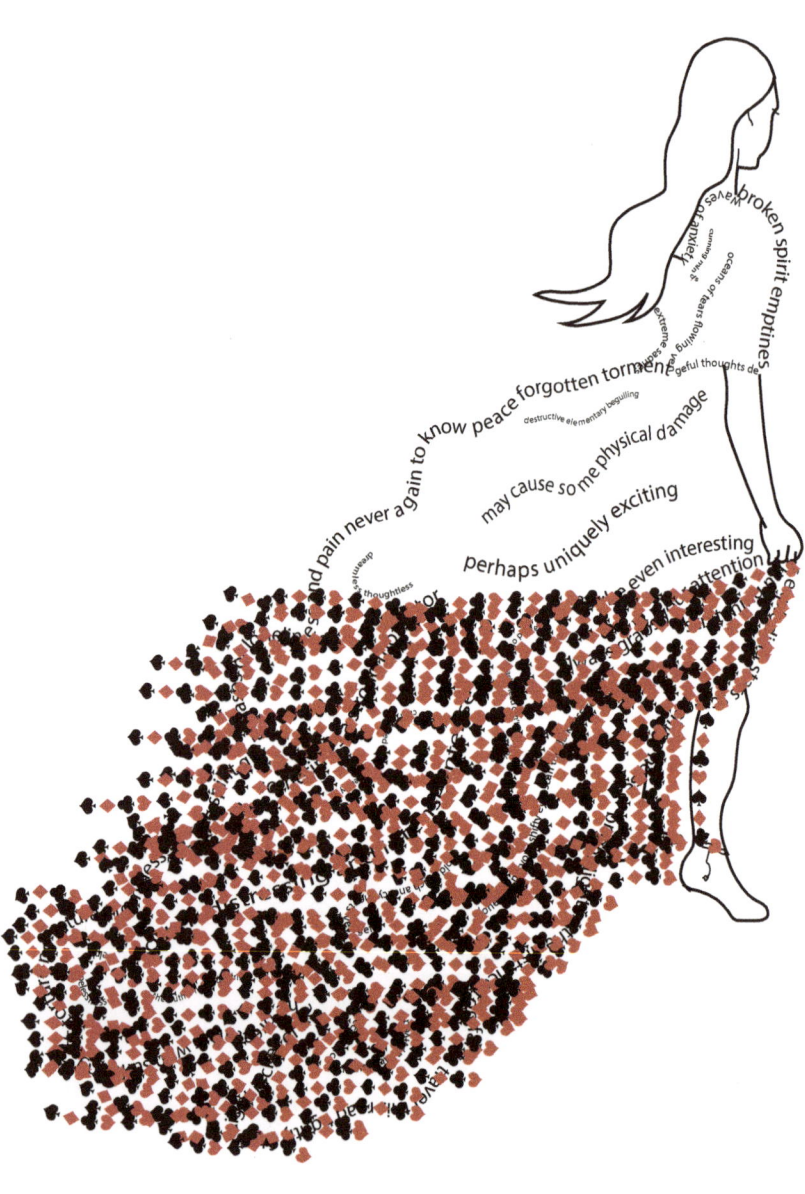

Humanity (Cont'd)

What about our children's future?
Our world is being poisoned
by murderous criminals—
    I hope we stop it in time.

Oh, where is our saviour?
Show us the way and
lead us not into temptation—
    annihilation is at hand.

Humans are survivors, right?
Mankind will find a way
if we only have faith—
    it's in our blood.

Can we all pull together?
We need to be actively involved
or our planet will die—
    we will die.

Will anyone help us?
We need swift and sure assistance
from someone with experienced wisdom—
    spirit and unity will be ours.

Where is our leader?
One who can teach us to survive
using our mind, body, and soul—
    life is precious.

Can you not see it?

Comfort Zone: Breaking Out

uncertainty rising
afraid of the road ahead
can't help looking back

Forget Me Not

Forget me not, is all I say
    Please mourn my sunken home
    People are now moved far away
The streets a catacomb

Fragmented house, it sways this way
    Upon the sand filled loam
    Forget me not, is all I say
Please mourn my sunken home

A tear for mem'ries of the day
    Of past and future tome
    The ghosts of Holland Island stay
Please mourn my sunken home.

Our Past and Future Selves

PAST
destructive, elementary
beguiling, exacting, appealing
simple, ostentatious, hateful, deceitful
deteriorating, polluting, killing
uncertain, bleak
FUTURE

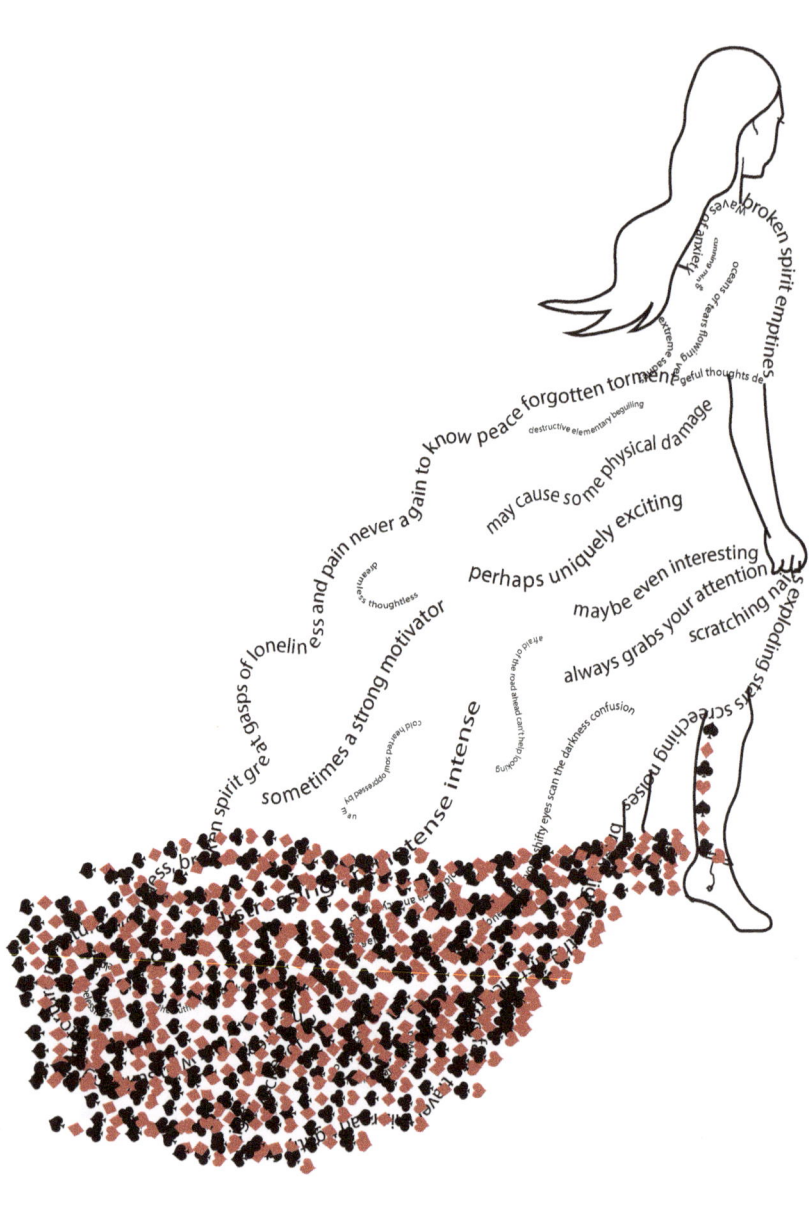

Bloodshot

black hole…
bloody, swollen, exploding
artwork on vision's canvas

War

Compelling men of arms anytime
Brothers and sisters for a lifetime

Brave souls, not just a paradigm
Marching toward goals in pantomime

Oh, but what life is so sublime
Drawn into the pit of wartime

Turbid and clear at the same time
A paradox of meaning and rhyme.

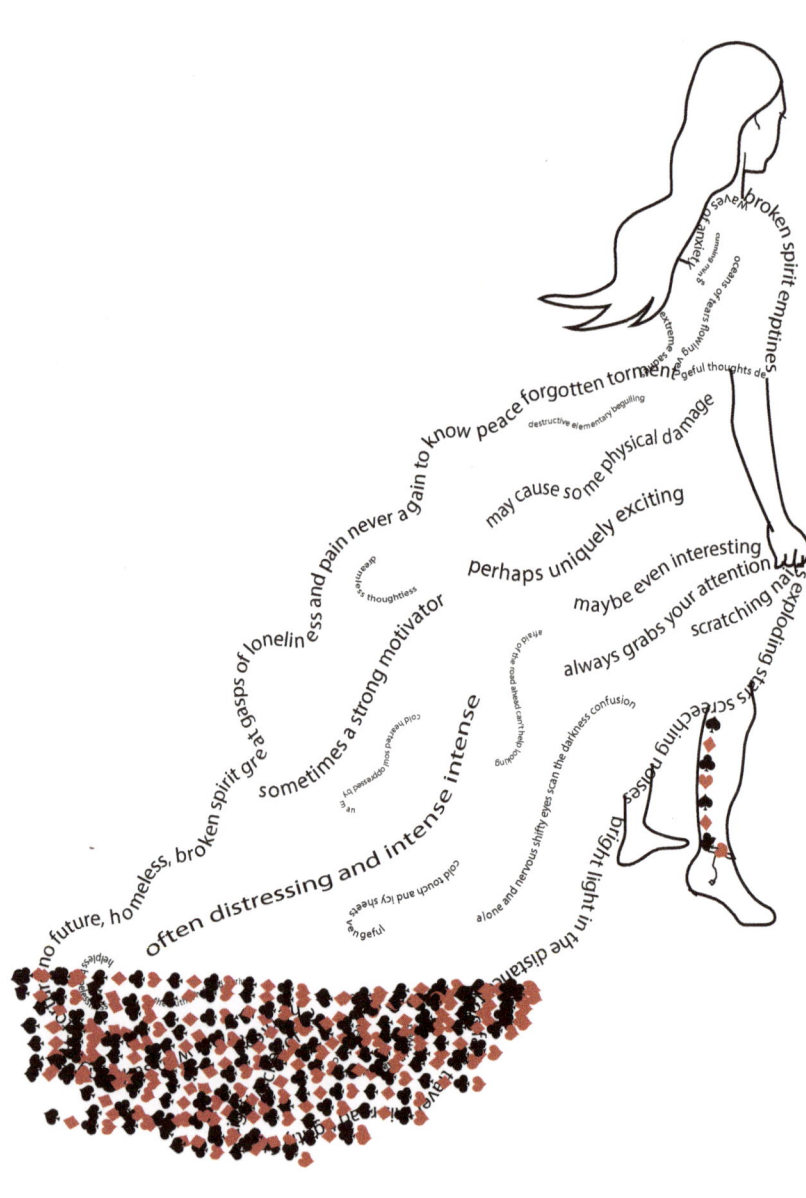

Mud

Miserable lane of depression
Undermining our prolific procession
Dilating our own aggression

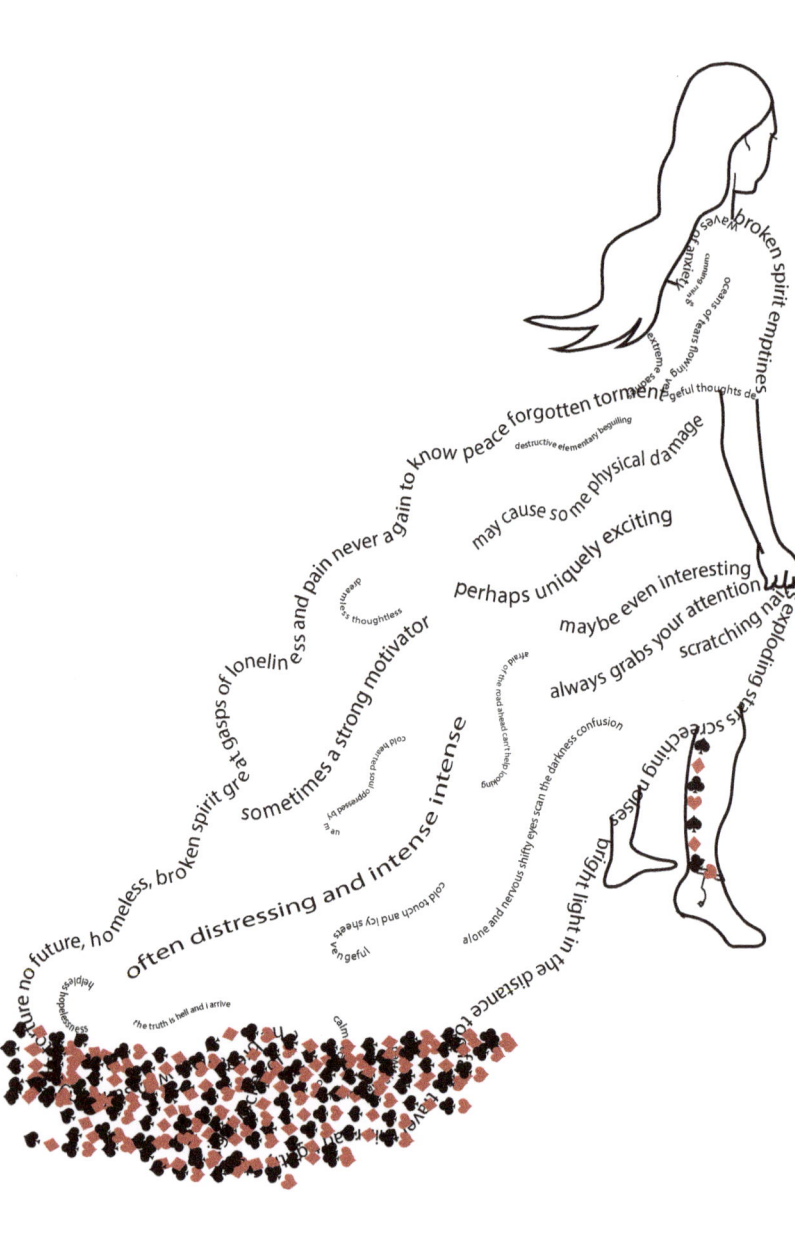

Perfectly Imperfect Woman

Adventurous and abusive as turbulent seas
Alluring as a siren's mad caterwaul
Annoyingly perfect artistic banshee
Wondrously awkward, an angelic fireball

She's foolish and feisty in perception
Her forgetfulness somewhat forgiving
Flirtatious and fickle, the exception
Although flawed in nature, fair at kissing

A bewitching bitch in the strictest sense
With brilliant displays of betrayal
Bubbly backstabbing, we're on the defense
A blessed, beguiling portrayal

Provocatively psychotic is her routine
After all, she can't help but be mean.

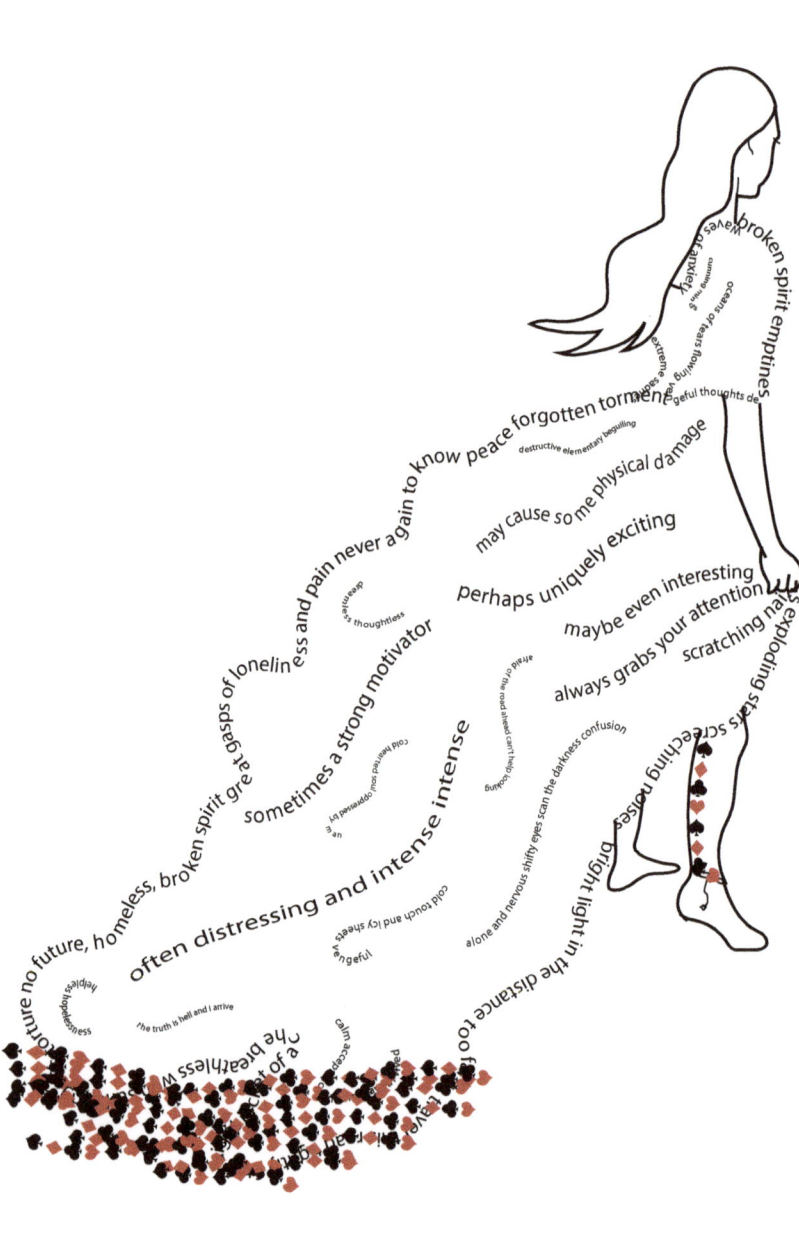

All is Not Lost

Echoes in our minds
Fate decrees its passage
Dread steals its way into our hearts
The time is here

Deception is present
From one soul to another
Long lost hope is too far away
He is here

Oh how wicked we are
Never to be true to each other
Our hearts and minds war engulfed
Turmoil here

We fall from clouds
Our lonely passage clear
Down, past remaining human life
The pit is here

Terror befalls us
Crawling, biting, ripping
Raping our flesh, devouring our souls
Death is here

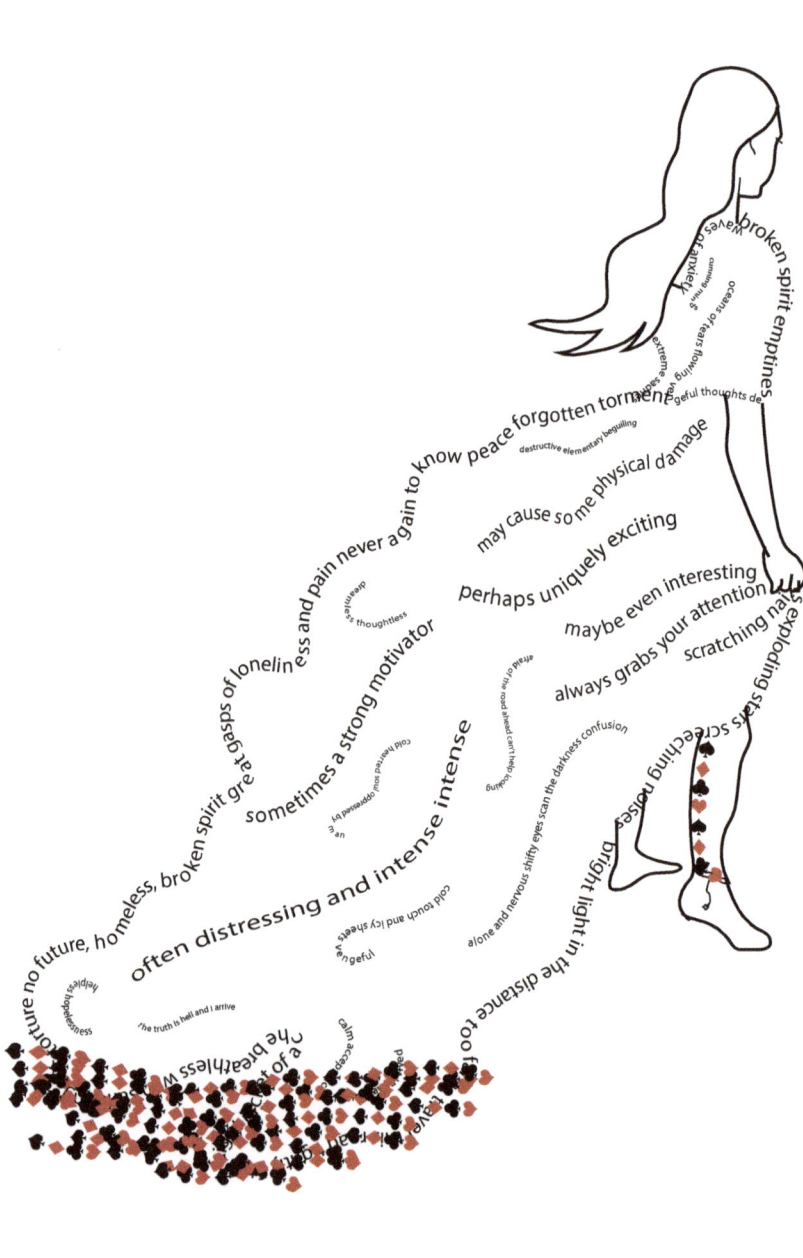

All is not lost (Cont'd)

We wail in agony
Surprised at the horrible truth
Sorrow takes hold and tears us apart
Redemption is here

Only He can save us
Resolute power absolute
We plead for compassion and mercy
Forgiveness is here

Light surrounds us
With strong mind and heart
We ascend to clouds, fearing nothing
Peace is finally here.

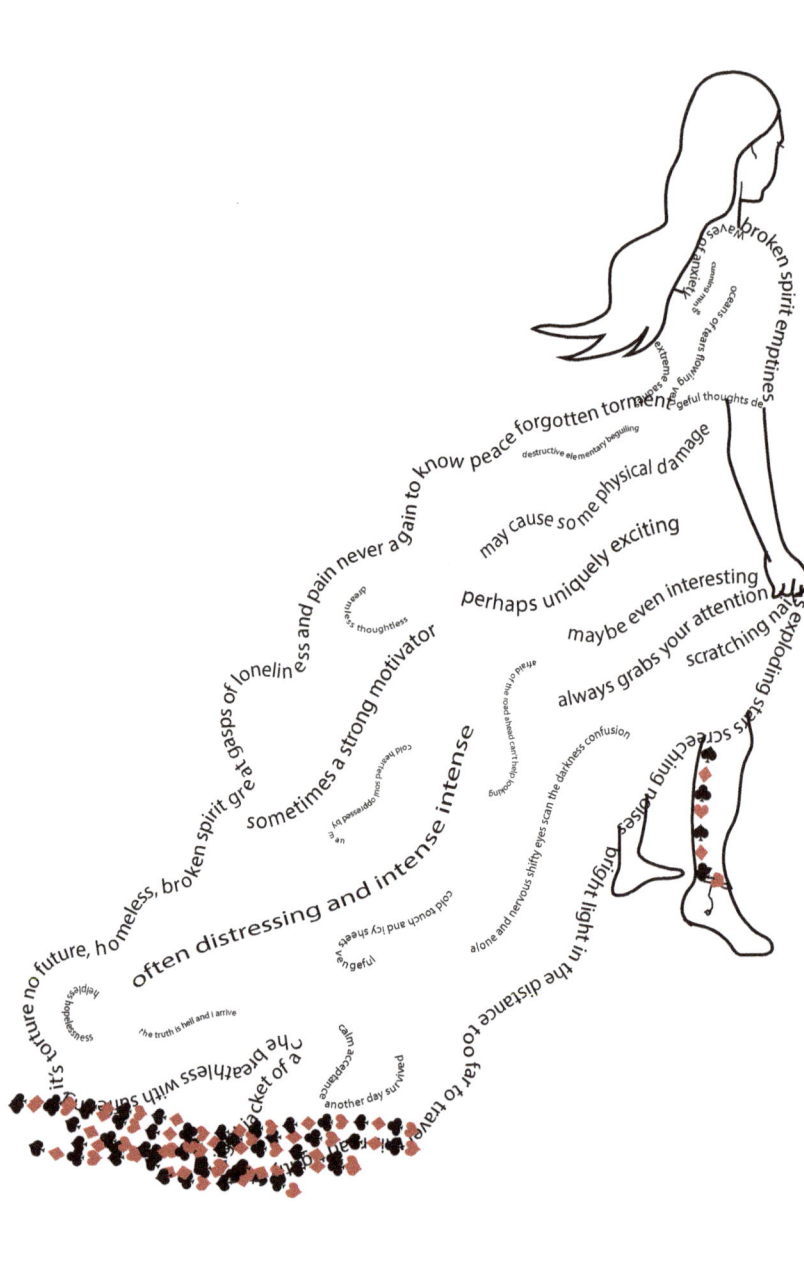

Our Pride and Joy

His heart is warmth and sunshine, true,
His body is earth and water so blue,
His spirit is young, a sweet gentle boy,
Our brother, our son, our pride and joy.

From heaven's gate we see him smile
And run and laugh and wave goodbye
"Don't cry!" he shouts, "today's the day
To live my life another way.

Think of me – a sparrow, a branch, a tree;
I'm in a better place, you see.
You'll see me maybe one day soon,
A part of earth, the stars, the moon.

Just take some dirt, a flower or leaf
And think of me and no more grief.
I'm happy, I'm healthy, and flying free—
Just say, 'see you later, honey bee'."

His heart is warmth and sunshine, true,
His body is earth and water so blue,
His spirit is young, a sweet gentle boy,
Our brother, our son, our pride and joy.

I Write

I write tonight because
                I feel the need.

I write tonight because
                the spirit calls.

I write tonight because
                my soul is freed.

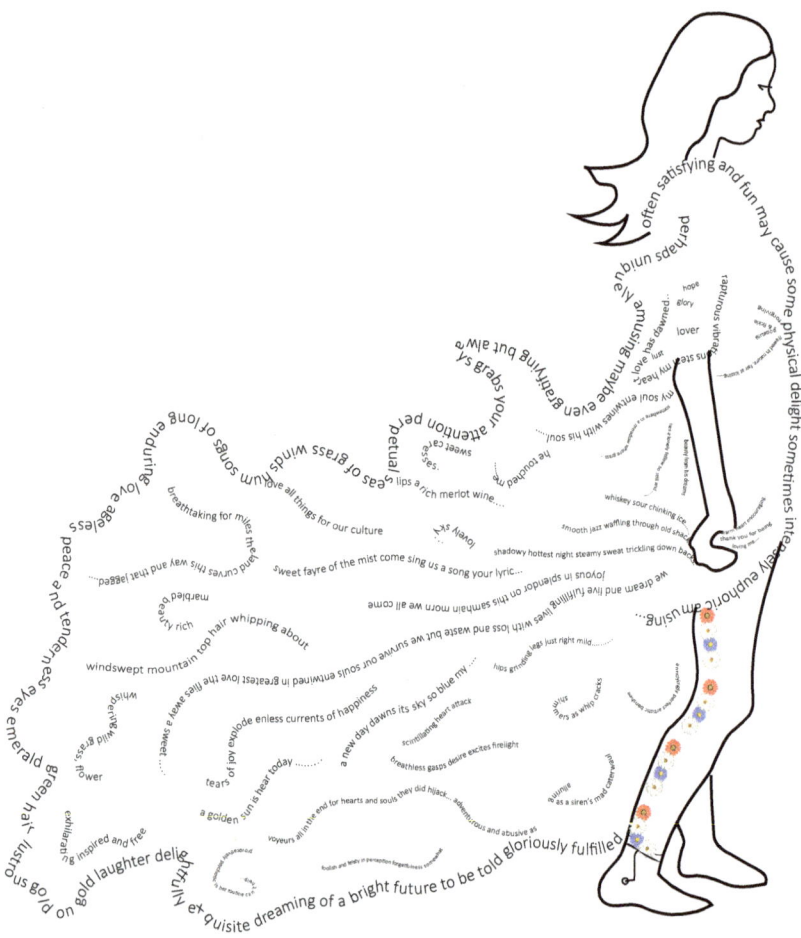

Chapter 2: Perception of Pleasure

Often satisfying and fun
May cause some physical delight
Sometimes intensely euphoric
Perhaps uniquely amusing
Maybe even gratifying
But always grabs your attention.

The Age

Walking through perpetual seas of grass
While winds hum songs of long enduring love,
Ageless peace and tenderness, it's made of—
Long ago, when I was but a wee lass.

Eyes emerald green, hair lustrous gold on gold,
Twirling through daisies, fair and delicate
With laughter delightfully exquisite—
Dreaming of a bright future to be told.

The life we lived, gloriously fulfilled,
Its message revealing a fairy tale song,
A wondrous moment to live for eons—
Love all things for our culture to rebuild.

Fayre

Sweet Fayre of the mist
Come sing us a song
Your lyric is such bliss
For us all who belong

Joyous in splendor
On this Samhain morn
We all come together
Exquisiteness born

Oh fairest of fair
With curls of spun gold
Your lilt of the angels
A story to unfold

We listen intently
And what do we hear
But songs we love plenty
For which will endure

We love you maid kind
And wish you good day
As you fly with the wind
And head home to the Fae.

Sens du Temps

tick-tock, tick-tock, tick-tock

anxious, eager, time seems
subtle and vague and mean
rarely enough, so lean
tick-tock, tick-tock, tick-tock

antique, haute-mode, it stands
pretty, ornate, slim bands
moving so slight its hands
tick-tock, tick-tock, tick-tock

so smooth, so clean, it shines
vibrate, pulsate, it rhymes
keeps track of all that time
tick-tock, tick-tock, tick-tock

walnut, cedar, rosewood
red oak, ash burl, plywood
cedar, balsam, all good
tick-tock, tick-tock, tick-tock

chords of noisette au beurre
apple, hard pear, allure
iron, metal, so pure
tick-tock, tick-tock, tick-tock

though all these things we know
somehow it's clear, although
the truth a clever gismo
with time a brief shadow

Sweet Dove

The time has come for you and I
To take our wings and say goodbye
As love and life forever hold
It's you and I together mold

Long life and prosperity
Are not a simple guarantee
One yields an honest heart and hope
To live and prosper within our scope

We dream and live fulfilling lives
With loss and waste, but we survive
Our souls entwined in greatest love
That flies away, a sweet, pure dove.

Mariovo's Immortal Voice

windswept mountain top
hair vigorously whips about
BREATHTAKING

carved land for miles
peaks and valleys abound
JAGGED MARBLED BEAUTY

rich history of ancient kings and war
trenches and spirits
HAUNTING VOICES

forgotten villages of stone and slate
time's heavy burden
MARIOVCI HEARTS REMAIN

jingle jangle, jingle jangle
"baaaah", says one – and so say all
SHEPHERD'S STAFF

ovci staring: who are you?
protectors at the ready
FIELDS OF LIFE

phantom loads of bundled hay
stogovi dot the land
MAGARINJA BRAYING

whispering wild grass and flowers
mosquitoes like birds
VALLEY OF ECHOES

tears of joy explode
endless currents of happiness
EXHILARATING

momentary stilled heart
one with the land
INSPIRED AND FREE

boundless emotions
ETERNAL.

Something New

It's bright one morn
That I did rise
And what is born
To my surprise

A golden sun
Is here today
Its rays abound
Are here to stay

My mind is clear
My hopes alive
I show no fear
As now I strive

For something new
And bright and warm
To melt the dew
On this fine morn

From far and wide
My search lies there
With greatest strides
I'll take good care

The sun sets low
As night draws near
I'll take a bow
And show no fear

A new day dawns
Its sky so blue
My heart is warm
For something new.

Affaire des Levres

If only I could find
A color so sublime…

Rose Quartz, Peacock Ore
Moonstone, I want more !

Brick Red, Sour Cherry
Red Velvet, drive me crazy !

Femme Fatale, Sexual Healing
Come Undone, oh what a feeling !

It keeps lips moist
What a perfect choice…

Aloe, Shea Butter
Beeswax, time to shiver !

Almond oil, Glycerin
Rose hip oil, usher in !

Cocoa butter, Jojoba
Argan oil, such a phobia !

…And what did I find
to help color these lips of mine
something so darn divine,
a rich merlot wine.

The Kiss

There in a meadow
where grass is so green
lies a lonely fellow
so still and serene

we see from afar
he looks fast asleep
and as we come near
there's still not a peep

a hat on his face
his feet are both crossed
awake? there's no trace
he snores like a hog

he dreams of true love
and sweet happiness
the things life's made of
not anything less

with eyes emerald green
blond curls on her head
her body so lean
and lips fiery red

sweet touch of heaven
from a pixie girl
does bring him awake
with her hair unfurled

he tips up his hat
and what does he see
a small fairy gnat
twirling down on he

around and around
at his side she goes
his dream is but found
he whispers "hello"

her breath near heaven
his heart beats so fast
she sighs
"here is your present"
her kiss meant to last.

The Dawning

As sweet as a whisper's soft caress
His hands did touch me
As passionate as his bold lust breaks
My soul entwines with his.

The moon rises above the heavens
To complete this moment of glory
Rapturous vibrations steal my heart
We fall from the clouds, exhausted.

As pure and innocent as we are still
Our hearts rejoice
As freedom flies within our breath
Love has dawned.

The Dance

moonlit
smudgy silhouettes
steamy sweat trickling down their backs

whiskey sour
chinking ice
smooth jazz waffling through the old shack

hips grinding
legs just right
mild scintillating heart attack

breathless gasps
desire excites
feverish minds on the right track

voyeurs all
in the end
for hearts and souls they did hijack

Still, the Waters Call

For miles the still ocean calls to me;
its voice clear,
clean,
empty.

"Why are you here?" it asks.

Why indeed.

"I've come to write among the waters," I answer.
"Life-giving and hearty, they are;
in hopes I will, too, gain that which is abundant."

"You are not one of us," it breathes heavily.

"True.
But I am also water:
can you not feel it?" I ask.

A pause. A gentle swell of waves.

"Come to us so that we may feel you," it says.
Nervous, anxious energy.

"Yes," I murmur.

My limbs descend into the silky fluid that is water;
my torso submerges.
Slow currents caress me.
I am home.

"We feel you," it says,
"Welcome."

Still, the Waters Call (Cont'd)

One last swirl and then calm:
Relief.
Tingles across my skin.

I'm in my boat again,
wet and reassured.
The hazy summer sun evaporates the ocean's lifeblood.
My mind is clear.

"I am inspired to write here, among you, the water," I say.

Wind shatters the silence.
Hair whips across my face.
Uneasiness creeps into my soul.

"You are not safe here," it says.

"But why? Why am I not safe?" I ask in confusion,
"You welcomed me."

My heart skips a beat, or two.

"Come another day," it urges.

Torment,
loneliness,
hurt,
regret,
hate.

Wave after wave of emotions
crash into my boat.

Still, the Waters Call (Cont'd)

I am capsized; sputtering to stay above water.

"GO NOW !" It screams.

How can I?
My boat is no longer afloat.

"I am alone in your lifeblood, water.
Tell me what to do !"

Icy fear liquefies my spine.
"Tell me what to do," I beg.

"Surrender yourself to me," it whispers.
Winds build to carry its message.

"Be part of me, one with me:
clean,
pure,
free," it entreats.

Cold dread turns me to stone.
I begin to sink.
"NO !" I blast.

Not today, not tomorrow, not ever.
I am what I am.
Why does it want to hurt me?

Anguish,
joy,
fulfillment,
flows around my body.

Still, the Waters Call (Cont'd)

It tugs at my legs,
pulls me down,
down,
down.

After a while, I am released.
I surface,
choking.

"Don't hurt me," I beg.

Stillness:
nothing but rippling waves for an eternity.
I am so tired.

"We are doing what we must," it finally says.

"Why ?" I cry.

I float on my back
staring up at the blue sky.
Water swirls under me,
around me.
Tears mingle with water.

"We are water," it says.
"You are water,
you are here."

"But I am not like you !" I cry.
"I can't be with you !"

Silence.
Uneasiness.

Still, the Waters Call (Cont'd)

"You were lying to us ?" it tentatively asks.

"YES !" I sob.
"I wanted to be like you, to fit with you, to know you !"

Confusion.
Annoyance.
"We are water, you are other," it says.

A blast of water near me.
My boat sits atop the water,
free and clear,
right side up.

I climb inside with
aching relief,
tears.

"Do not pretend to be us," it says,
"You are not like us,
we are not like you."

"I won't," I promise,
"I won't."

I grab the oars and begin to row.
Back to shore;
back to safety.

My journal sits on the seat in front of me:
Dry and open to the first page.
A drop of water the only entry.

I grab my shirt to wring it out, but it is dry.

Still, the Waters Call (Cont'd)

I look up to the sky.
The sun casts a farewell glance,
black clouds in the distance.

A flock of seagulls cry.
Laughing from somewhere close.
The savory smell of hickory smoked barbecue
tantalizes my senses.

A glance to my right:
the dock is beside me,
the boat tied off.
I am still here.

Realization sets in.
I haven't left the dock.

My hand trails aimlessly in the water.
Cool flowing liquid.
Young weeds surface, brush my hand.

"Thank you," I whisper in reverence,
a glance at the foreboding blackness in the sky.

I pick up my journal and climb onto the dock.

"Another day," I say to the water.

A wave crashes into the dock;
a small spray of water kisses my face.

"Yes," it says,
"another day."

I Write

I write today because
>> my mind is compelled.

I write today because
>> my body is free.

I write today because
>> my soul is fulfilled.

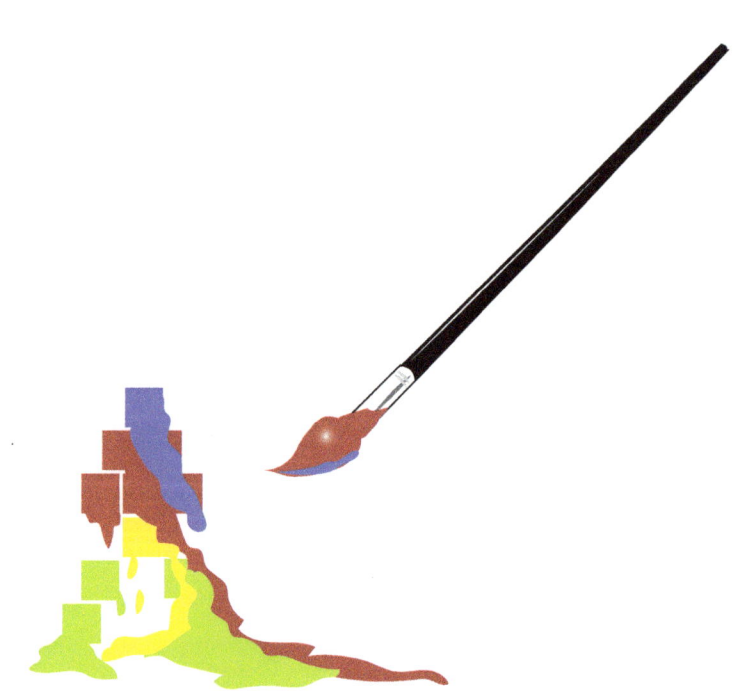

Chapter 3: Thought

Often random in nature

May cause moments of exhilaration

Sometimes deeply meditative

Perhaps uniquely imperfect

Maybe even impressive

But always an artist's stroke

on

mind's canvas.

Jeweled Pair

Crystalline focus…
fairy's rainbow at
Neverland's gate

Feet: What Stories They Tell

Jamboree…
scuba diving in ocean's
wide mouth

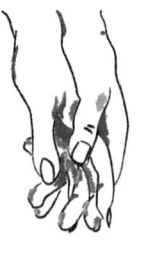

Found

Rapturous moments
Majestic in time's embrace
In peace, we are found

Summer's Dream

twinkles in heaven's blanket
    over the moon…
        nightlight

The Beach

silver bangles...
passionate embrace
of peaceful sands

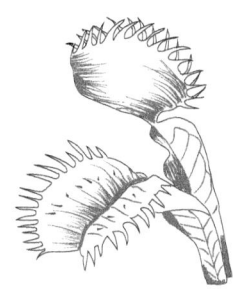

Venus Fly Trap

nectar...
lovely melody of
umeboshi

Abandon

Flood of excitement
Adrenaline pumps wildly
Eternally free

Corn Dog Grass

...erection

intrepidly proliferates then
withers and dies

Last Night Being Single

matrimony...

       surprising sorrow at love's

            yearning gate

Honey

reflective moonlight
washes your skin in honeyed
tones of pure delight

Aiko's Nest

Glorious nectar

Scintillating and glossy
Abundantly keen

Little Monster

cookies…
blow in my mouth to create
a little more room

Love in the After-World

Forgotten rapture
Desiccated, buried soul
Singular glory

Supernatural Gloss

entombed—
fire breathing dragons captured
by cold calculated time

Forever Entwined

Madness touches me
　Flowing in my lover's arms
　　Still, in time's moment

Garden

coalesced droplets
meandering down stained-glass…
joyous reunion

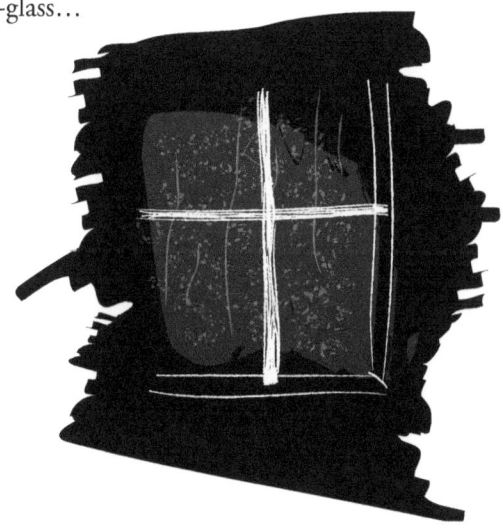

Eau de Redolence

sweet notes of
tuberose fill the air…
flatulence

soft and light like
fresh laundry in the barnyard…
Vieux Boulogne

old man's cottage…
transfixed by time and
empty shadows

Buried in Vines

Holiday

adventure…
crushed shells in life's
empty glass

Full

Good life for our helpful, hopeful kind
Present is our dreamful, thoughtful mind
Hopeful
Helpful
Dreamful
Thoughtful

Take-Away Thought

Never give up on your dreams...

In the blink of an eye

and twirling of snow flake streams,

a fortuitous goodbye

may light a path so bright, it seems

to your mind's eye

brings glorious sunbeams.

Artwork on Mind's Canvas

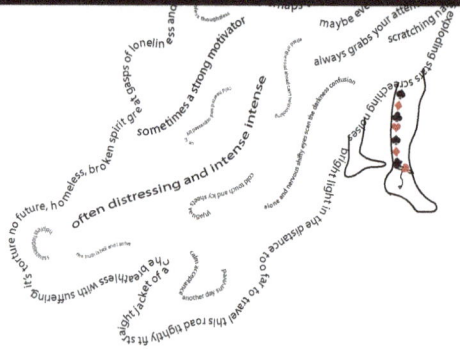

About the Author

Artwork on Mind's Canvas is Shelley Ann Vrgleski's debut illustrated book of poetry. She lives in Ontario, Canada.

www.shelleyannvrgleski.com

www.ingramcontent.com/pod-product-compliance
Lightning Source LLC
Chambersburg PA
CBHW040336300426
44113CB00021B/2760